*Praise For*

# Exceptional: The Inspired Words
# of Middle School Poets

**"Your words are indeed magic. Let them be read out loud!"**

– Florence Parry Heide, the award-winning author of more than
 sixty children's books, including the classics: *The Shrinking of Treehorn,
 Treehorn's Treasure and Treehorn's Wish*

**"Readers will find much to admire in these many playful
and joyous poems that sparkle with the delight and wonder
of the world keenly observed through the unique perspective
of 6th grade poets."**

– Richard Hedderman, Milwaukee Public Museum Poetry Competitions
 Coordinator/Lead Judge

# Exceptional: The Inspired Words of Middle School Poets

**By 6th Grade Middle School Class
of St. Joseph Catholic Academy**

Kenosha, Wisconsin
2009-2010

**Coconut Avenue,® Inc.**
Chicago, Illinois USA

# Table of Contents

# Forward

Sixth grade students in middle school are such a joy to spend the day with! As a seasoned teacher, it is an immeasurable gift to be able to challenge young, inquiring minds as they attempt to show us, the adults around them, how they see the world. As we journey through each school year, I am amazed by their enthusiasm, curiosity and ability to comprehend information as they increase their skill level. It is often similar to a flood light suddenly beaming. At the moment a concept is first understood, especially if a student struggles, he or she immediately changes facial expression and body language. I often wish parents could be with us during the day to see this transformation.

When we began writing poems this fall each student researched a subject for the "ancient artifacts" assignment. The holiday poems were created with each student's "favorites" in mind. We laughed, sighed and shed a few tears over the sentimentality of some. As each student read his or her poem to the class it was interesting to watch the faces of their classmates register appropriate emotions and understanding.

# Forward

I am thankful for the opportunity to share and grow with these hard working and intuitive young people. Each day with them renews my faith in mankind and assures me our country's future is bright with citizens like these fine young men and women to lead us in this crazy world in which we live today.

**Mary Robinson**
*6th Grade Language and Writing Teacher*

St. Joseph Catholic Academy
Kenosha, Wisconsin
May 2010

# 6th Grade Poets 2009-2010

*St. Joseph Catholic Academy*
*Kenosha, Wisconsin*

# Book Cover Contest

All of the 6th Grade poets were also encouraged to submit an original work of art that could potentially be used for the cover of this book. The submitted works of art were collected and evaluated by the middle school faculty.

The original work of art submitted by Miss Lindsey Thomas was selected to be used as the cover of the student book of poetry. Congratulations to Miss Thomas!

It was the decision of the publisher to include Miss Thomas's artwork inside this book and use an alternative cover to allow this book to potentially generate as much revenue as possible for the scholarship fund created by the students.

# Book Cover Contest Winner

*Ms. Lindsey Thomas*

# Poems

# Charleston

*by Alex Ambro*

Our trip to Charleston was very fun
It was colder than we expected.
We did many exciting things,
Such as go to the beach and smell the ocean breeze.
And feel the sand in our toes
On those cold days in Charleston.

We went to Fort Sumter, which is very old.
But it is very well preserved.
It still has cannon ball marks on the walls.

We went to see the city,
And stood on the same sea battery that Charlestonians
Stood on to watch the Battle of Fort Sumter rage on.

That is what we did on vacation,
I hope you enjoyed.
Our trip to Charleston was very fun.

# The Nazca Lines

*by Alex Ambro*

The Nazca Lines are in Peru,
They probably could not be read by you.
The Nazca Lines were made very oddly,
They were made by removing stones!
The Nazca Lines are so large,
They can only be read by the gods.
Definitely not from a barge.

# Mummies

*by Kate Anthony*

Mummies are freaky
Mummies are creepy
Mummies can even be sneaky
Mummies can't talk
But they surely can walk
So don't let those mummies give you a scare
Keep an eye out they're everywhere.

# Baker Street

*by Kate Anthony*

My favorite restaurant is Baker Street
They have delicious food.
My mom and dad, brothers and I
Eat there all the time.
My favorite breakfast foods are their large omelets
And the variety of fruit you can put on your crepes
like cherry and apple.
They have soda, slushies, milk and root beer floats.
My favorite drink is the strawberry slushies
They always put an orange on a rim.
I'll never forget that my favorite restaurant is
Baker Street!

# Runes

*by Geoffrey Bennett*

Runes are cool
But try not to drool
Read a rune
Set your mind a brewing
What will your future bring?

# The Christmas Light

*by Geoffrey Bennett*

I went to watch
The Christmas light
In its final hour of bright

I watch the glow of
The Christmas light darken
as if you saw the
sun go down

the clock hit midnight
and the light
of the Christmas light
was replaced with the
darkness of night.

# The Tasty Hamburger

*by Dylan Boyd*

My uncle bought a calf.
I named her Dakota.
Dakota lived for many years in a field that had her
droppings and that smelled like a dump.
One day she became very sick and we didn't want her
to suffer. So my uncle had her butchered and my cousin
bought some meat.
My grandpa and I visited by cousin and
we stayed for dinner.
He made some hamburgers and they were huge but tasty.
I could smell and hear the grilled onions sizzle and the
meat cooking like a five star restaurant.
The burgers were good so in return we made strawberry pie.
You could smell the fresh berries.
They loved and so did I.

He made some hamburgers and they were huge but tasty.
I could smell and hear the grilled onions sizzle and the
meat cooking like a five star restaurant.
The burgers were good so in return we made strawberry pie.
You could smell the fresh berries.
They loved and so did I.

# Gladiators

*by Dylan Boyd*

Gladiators are the most ferocious men in the world
They will fight until they're dead.

The Coliseum they call home and resting place
They will show respect to the Roman king.

"We who are about to die salute you!"
Words that are said before the death match.

# Greek Architecture

*by Joe Carney*

Your architecture leaves me amazed,
Your architecture leaves architects crazed.

You were made eons ago,
You lasted through rain, sleet and snow.

You were designed to show we've come so far,
Now we have the bike, plain, train and car.

You're big, bad and all that, for sure
Oh yeah, you're Greek architecture.

# The Economy

*by Joe Carney*

The economy,
Is up and down,
North and south,
It's all around.

Like a bullet the gas price goes up,
Right with our high strung tempers.
Then we start to think,
Will we join those poor homeless people?

The depression is back, strong as before,
As though it wants revenge.
While it swipes away our money,
We lose all hope to reclaim our jobs.

The economy,
Is up and down,
North and south,
It's all around.

# The Toy Train

*by Luz Chavez*

It was a cold December day,
I saw something bright.

On Christmas lane,
It was a big candy cane.

Right next to it was a toy train,
With headlights.

The owners must have been bright,
To decorate all the lights.

I saw some carolers they looked like elves,
They played a song with bells.

The train also made puffs of smoke,
Every time it took a stroke.

The smoke smelled like strawberries,
It was really astonishing.

I will never forget that day,
That cold December day.

# The Lost City of Pompeii

*by Luz Chavez*

If Mount Vesuvius hadn't blown its top,
Pompeii wouldn't have had a stop.

While Pompeii was being buried,
People tried to get out in hurry.

If you were there you would have thunk,
Did the people go bonkers?

Pompeii was found after all these years,
So now you can see it for a mere $17.50.

# The Great Wall of China

*by Kaitlin Christoun*

The Great Wall of China
Where many people go.
It was built to protect its land
From enemies and foes.
A dancing dragon in the starry night
Even the pictures of this wall are beautiful sights.
Many years ago people were buried in this wall
No matter how tired these people were they still built the wall tall.

# Chocolate Cake

*by Kaitlin Christoun*


I shove down lots of chocolate cake,
But not as much as I like!
Eating it quickly with my fork,
Food flying left and right!

All over the floor is a lot of cake,
It's covered up my cats.
There's cake on the chair and in my hair.
The walls are all chocolately splats

Faster and faster I eat it up,
With chocolate all over my milk cup.
As it's all over the place and on my face,
A drop of frosting falls off my nose and goes plop.

Now it's all gone it was not enough,
I need much more to eat.
I look around the room and smile,
There I spot Hershey bars in a pile.

# Christmas Lights

*by Liz Collins*

Christmas Lights
Small but bright, and light up the trees at night.
From blue to yellow to green to pink
And some even blink.

They lay on the trees, flowing in the breeze.
And don't make a sound, while some fall to the  ground.

Make the perfect decoration for some occasions.
Christmas Lights.

# The Great Wall of China

*by Chloe Crowe*

Miles and miles of history,
He wall connects China's past to its future.
It took 2,000 years for men to complete.
The world is amazed by it,
The Chinese are proud of it.
If only it could reveal all of its mysteries.

# Jets Skiing

*by Matthew Curry*

The beaches are smooth
The water is cold
But that doesn't stop me from
Having fun

The jet skis are speedy
The waves are crashing
But that doesn't stop me from
Having fun

The waves are hitting me so hard
It is hard to have some fun
But the jet skis and I are
Best of friends

When you dock your body begins to shake
Like a baby's rattle
But that won't stop me from getting on again.
Get a bite to eat. Get a little rest then hit the waves
Again.

Hear hear, the waves go by crashing into you.
But that doesn't stop me from having fun.

# You Never Know

*by Matthew Curry*

Some have been afraid, some have
Been curious, and some don't care.
But yes this is the mummy. Many
Stories have been told about the
Mummy. Nothing to be afraid of
Except bodies. Try to get close and
You might be afraid. It might have
A smile but don't let it fool you, but
These mummies can do what you
Want them to.

# Fruits

*by Kate DelSavo*

Fruits.
Some fruits are round.
Some are found.
Underneath kid's bed.
Fruits.

Fruits
Strawberry
Orange
Pineapple
Oh My!
Fruits

Fruits
I love fruits!
Can't you tell?
Maybe I'll be swell.
If all we have to eat,
Is fruit
I love fruits.

Fruits
When will the day
Come when we all
May
Have fruits to eat
Fruits.

# The Pig Dig

*by Luke Dickow*

When I went to the pig dig
I found some bones as small as twigs.
There were some bones
In-between all the stones.
Put them all together, they make up the pig.

When I was done digging I used the brush
I swore I heard the pig say "shush."
As I came back to my house
I was scared as a mouse.
Thinking that I was the pig.

# Christmas Tree

*by Luke Dickow*


Families wandering around the forest,
cutting the large trees down until there are none left.
People enjoying the memories they had,
decorating the trees with ornaments, garland, lights.

Presents at the tree base on Christmas morning.
Children filled with joy,
excited to see what they've received.

Decorated with ornaments, garland, lights.
Green grass, large as the sea, prickly as though it is a porcupine.
With a glowing gold star on top,
sometimes with candy canes scattering the branches.

Christmas tree.

# The Sea

*by Stefani Fallabeck*

Water and Sand
Are parts of the sea.

With blue open sky
It's an awesome place to be.

Try to have fun while in the sun
But never give up before the day is done

Try to imagine the sea
Or write it down.

Go up toward the sea
You won't drown

Once again
I might add

Water and sand
Are parts of the sea.

# The Stonehenge

*by Stefani Fallabeck*

Has more than nine hundred stone rings,
I have heard so many things.

The stones are great,
But it is very out of date.

A wooden sanctuary in the middle,
And it is not very little.

To me, it looks like a dream world,
The Stonehenge is a wonder of the ancient world.

# The Seashore

*by Cecilia Grinis*

On the beach, I lay in the hot sand
The waves bristle against my feet
Like a paintbrush in an artist's hand.

On the beach, my brother makes
A sandcastle that is hard to break
Until a large dog starts running free
Oh, how sad my brother would be.

The seashore is a great place to relax
It is not an opinion, it's a fact! Knowing if I
Should play or should I sleep
The seashore is a great place to be.

# Pompeii

*by Cecilia Grinis*


As I walked through the villa,
I felt a sudden rumble
I ran outside and saw rocks tumble
Vesuvius had just erupted
People were running all around town
As Pompeii was falling down.

As the lava kept flowing
The terror kept growing
We ran to the sea
But the ash we could not flee
Then at last
Came the poison gas

Pompeii was destroyed...
As so was I.

# Injuries

*by Nathan Ilada*

Ouch, snap, clonk, break, slap
It happens everywhere just look on the map
Look out is could be you
Punch! Ouch it just turned blue!
Be careful so you don't get hurt
Oh no it just scratched my shirt!
Be alert before it could happen
Clonk there goes John Madden
Kaboom! There you go and now you know
Have fun, but take it slow.

# The Great Pyramid

*by Mariesa Jones*

Egyptians, Egyptians, a culture obsessed
With dying and death and much, much distress.
Believed death would wander to the next world.
Buried with rubies and diamonds and pearls.
Lying in tombs housed in upside down cones.
These are called pyramids, which are made out of stone.
If you ever go to Egypt, make sure you stop by
To see the building that reaches the sky.

# Flu Shot

*by Mariesa Jones*

Sitting there
In the waiting Room
Waiting for your name
To be
Called in
The room with

The string of
Metal
Nervously staring
At the door
Patiently
Listening to
Weeping and
Whining of
Children
In pain
Gently trembling

In the wooden
Chair with
Leather cushions
Sudden
An unexpected
Voice
Calls my name
Palms sweaty
A tap
On the shoulder
And a hold
Of a hand
Calms
Me as I
Walk into a
Bright and unusual
Place with
Lots of strange.

# Jonas Brothers Concert

*by Dana Kuyawa*

A young lady wakes up very early on concert day
waking her dad by screaming HIP HOP Hooray it's
Jonas Brothers concert day!

Dad pleads for just a little more sleep as he covered his
head with the sheets. His Excited daughter began to weep.

Soon the duo was on their way. Written on the back of
the van was honk if you love the Jonas Brothers today!

Ned's pizza was a tradition for lunch for the cheese, sausage
and pepperoni is what they love a bunch.

Dad being goofy spilled his pop and his daughters'
laughter was hard to stop!

Near the concert the duo went it was on souvenirs
that big money was spent.

As the concert started their cheers grew loud, watching his
daughter rock with the Jonas Brothers made dad proud.

With the concert seeming to have just begun, before they
knew it the wonderful concert was done.

Jonas Brothers thanked their fans for wonderful night;
this band's popularity is quite a sight.

For daughter and daddy it was a perfect night.
As the dad drove home he smiled at his beautiful daughter
sleeping to his right.

# Mummies

*by Dana Kuyawa*

Mummies wrapped up so tight
As to protect them from the damaging light.
At first they buried their dead in coffins underground.
Finding out later the remains were not to be found.
This process of wrapping the dead is called mummification.
As to protect the dead from decomposition.
Egyptian amulets, oriental charms were worn by the dead.
Protecting them from what has not yet been said.
I think mummies are very creepy and at times rather kooky.
Leaving me with thoughts of mummies that are very spooky.

# Hamburgers

*by Ryan Landgraf*

I love hamburgers.
They are always made
On a grill with stinky
Charcoal. You might like ketchup,
Mustard, hot lily, tasty mayo,
Crunchy lettuce, or sour tomato.
The meat will be so juicy.
I really don't like the disgusting
Burnt pieces. It will really hurt if your
Hand gets burnt on the grill.
The hamburger is so tasty when the cheese
Is melted onto the warm burger.
All of the ingredients look like a rainbow.
I love hamburgers.

# The Great Wall of China

*by Ryan Landgraf*

The Great Wall of China is very long.
The Great Wall of China winds like a song.

It is very tall and
Makes you feel small.

As you walk across this great big wall,
It's amazing that man could make it at all.

It stretches for miles: farther than you can see,
It disappears in the distance far away from me.

Built many years ago of earth and stones
The wall is stronger than all of your bones.

# Great Wall

*by Brooke Leonardo*

The Great Wall runs very long.
The Great Wall is big and strong.
It is a very good sight to see.
The Great Wall is where you want to be.
So why not visit
So you can see a bit of history.

# Roses

*by Brooke Leonardo*

Roses blow in the wind.
And settle in the moonlight ... roses
Roses are beautiful in every way.
You can see them in the grass while you lay ... roses

Roses can be given to a loved one.
Or a friend you care for ... roses
Getting one rose on an ordinary day
Is like getting twice as many presents on Christmas day ... roses

I love seeing a white powdery layer of snow on a rose
But once you get into winter things change and everybody knows
... roses.

# Cheese

*by Zachary Lesavich*


Cheese
is fun cheese is gooey
Cheese makes me happy.
Cheese can make anyone smile
Cheese is also chewy.

Cheddar I eat with a cola
Swiss I use on my sandwich
Blue cheese is very cool
And so is gorgonzola.

Cheese is Oh so tasty
Cheese is very good
Cheese looks very funny
Cheese tastes better than a pastry.

# The Old Days

*by Zachary Lesavich*

The old days were very hard.
For some people,
there weren't many possessions back then,
such as computers, games, and ipods.

Now it's 2010.
and many things have been made,
but what happened when,
these things didn't exist back then?

# Mummies

*by Elizabeth Lesperance*

Mummies old with tattered wraps
Lying in the desert pyramids.
Bodies are emptied, organs in jars
Awaiting an afterlife.
Decorations and precious gems
Lie in the quiet tombs.
Cats embalmed and buried with their masters
Awaiting glory or doom.
Hieroglyphics tell the stories of these mummies
And their guests.
Some that were never met.
Many stories are told of King Tutankhamun
How he lived and how he died.
All of them are questioned especially, why he met his death.
Mummies hold the keys to past lives.
They unlock history.
Why mummies are now looked at as scary in movies
Remains a mystery.

# Christmas is Almost Here

*by Elizabeth Lesperance*

Christmas is near
I have decorations to bring cheer
I have shopping to do
Christmas is near
I have to do my homework
I have clothes to pick out
Christmas is near
I have a tree to decorate with a star
I have to write my Christmas cards
Christmas is near
I need to pick out the lights
I need to pull the garland tight
Christmas is near

I need to to get the ornaments
That almost look like clouds of color
I have to bake the ham
And the big juicy lamb
Christmas is near
I have to get the presents wrapped
I have to get the sleeping bags out
Christmas is near
I have to make the cookies
I have to shovel the driveway from snow
And I have to go to bed
Christmas is here.

# Mummies

*by John Matteucci*

Well preserved and on their way,
the afterlife is where they'd stay.
Ancient Egyptians felt this to be so,
their dead were bandaged from head to toe.
Every mummy wrapped just right,
each strip of cloth placed around them tight.
These mummies all would soon be carried,
and placed in tombs their bodies buried.
Some with wealth and jewels galore,
the afterlife would open its door.
The mummy now, wrapped up real neat,
the passage is done the process complete.

# Milwaukee Public Museum Poetry Competition Award Winner 2010

In conjunction with its special exhibition: *Dead Sea Scrolls and the Bible: Ancient Artifacts, Timeless Treasures*, March-June 2010, the Milwaukee Public Museum sponsored a poetry competition for elementary, middle school and high school students from grades 3 through 12.

*Mummies*, by John Matteucci was selected as an award winning poem for this competition.

# Basketball

*by John Matteucci*

I was on the court today,
My mom told me to go and play.
So even though I'm not too tall,
I tried to shoot a basketball.
I bounced it fast and shot it strong,
But I saw the ball go long.
I grabbed it back for one more try,
I could tell that ball would fly.
I saw the hoop and went to aim,
Hey, I think this is my game.
The ball went up, I saw it spin,
And suddenly, that ball went in.

# First Snow

*by Alison Meeker*

Snow on my eyelashes
I'm bundled up tight
Cheeks are all rosy
I'm ready to fight.
The first snowball goes flying
It sails past my ear.
I come out of hiding
To whistle and cheer.
Another comes sailing
It misses by a mile.
The next one I throw
It makes me smile.
First snow of the season
It is a good reason
To have a snowball fight
So bundle up tight.

# Take A Walk With A Mummy

*by Alison Meeker*

Take a walk with a mummy and what will you see?
Tons of surprises waiting for you and for me!
You will discover adventure through the hieroglyphics
of ancient times.
Play a game of mancala with a pharaoh or scribe.
You may stop to pray in a temple or take a camel ride.
Look to the top of a pyramid or to the bottom of a tomb.
Learn about Egyptian numbers or paintings on the walls.
Take a walk with a mummy and you will see,
Many wonderful discoveries preserved for you and for me.

# The Moon

*by Elizabeth Mitchell*

The moon is bright
It gives great light.

Whenever I see
The moon gazing at me
I think of the endless possibilities
To be with the moon.

When I see the moon
It looks like a ball with holes

With the moon in the sky
I catch it
In my hands
And keep it always

In winter's night
Its snow white
In summer the moon is never shone
It's just being alone.

I love the moon when it came
To me; it belongs to the
World and me.

# The Great Wall

*by Elizabeth Mitchell*

This Great Wall
Pure and tall
Is the one looking for a time,
It doesn't cost a dime
To be a wall
With tile, and cement
You're a time worth spent
To be a wall
For people to die
You are a great try
To be a wall.

# Lost But Not Yet Found

*by Mary Nevin*

I am here
In a dark place
With a chapstick, a wallet
Hand sanitizer, trident gum
You have seven texts plus two missed calls
Look in the dark chamber of your
Possessions. I miss having my
Buttons pressed with your
Smooth hands. -I miss having
My screen massaged with
Your thumb that is so
Gentle and delicate
People are trying to contact you, the number
Of messages plus calls accumulates by the
Minute you currently have three missed
Calls, nine texts and one voicemail.

# Mummy

*by Mary Nevin*

A mummy is no dummy
History he tells
Of ancient times
And desert chimes
With stolen treasure wells.

# Missing

*by Nick Norris*

My original poems are missing.
Somehow they were lost.
Maybe they were stolen by a crook.
So I could be included, I wrote a new missing poem for this book.

# Three Words

*by Will Pechous*

The first word you might find easy
But don't be too mean and sleazy
This word is used a lot
The word is My.

The second work you might think is cool
Because it has synonyms like huge, giant humongous
and gianormous
The work is Big.

The next word you like a lot
Because you might have one or you might not
The word is Brother.

Put these three words together and you get
My Big Brother
He's cool, kind and everything else
Not to mention mean and not nice
But he's still by big brother and I love him.

# Hieroglyphics

*by Will Pechous*


Some predict devastation
One devastation for every nation
Or
Some speak of peace
Even though the peace is not what we have achieved
Or
Some are used for counting
Maybe someone was in accounting
But
When put together they make messages or war,
Life, death, and even our future.

# Breakfast Meal

*by Joseph Pounders*

You can eat this for breakfast, lunch or dinner.

You can add anything to it but eggs are key
As it cooks on the stove, it will taste good, you'll see.

The smells are great, coming from the pan
Because I used eggs, milk and even some ham.

Now that it is done, you must let it rest,
That way when you eat it, it will taste the best.

# Christmas

*by Joe Putz*

Christmas is coming,
I hope you've been good.
Drummers are drumming,
You know that they should.

It's getting much colder,
Start gathering wood.
Snows landing on shoulder,
Better put up my hood.

Wrapping a present,
Just to get ripped.
It is so pleasant,
Drinking cocoa that's whipped.

Christmas is coming,
Non-believers beware.
Angel's harp is strumming,
The messiah is here.

# Hebior Mammoth

*by Joe Putz*

In a township named Paris
At the edge of a field
They found a bone to cherish
But not typical of a farm
It was not from a cow, chicken or pig
What could they do but continue to dig?
A family named Hebior
With strong roots in farming
Found a skeleton to treasure
Without much warning
 Every piece put away
Told a story of long ago
It would need a home someday
And a grand place to show
The Milwaukee museum wanted this creature
To give a proper home
The Hebior Mammoth would be a feature
And look as it did when it roamed.

# Sky

*by Victor Ramierez*

Lying on my back, staring at the sky
I saw clouds bumping, billowing by
They were white, black, gray and red-orange
I left the field and wet to school
My mind stayed with the clouds because it was cool
I returned lying on my back, staring at the sky
I saw clouds bumping, billowing by.

# Mummies

*by Monica Rasch*

Mummies, mummies, mummies
Where did they all go?
They're sticky
They're slimy
What else is there to know?
They can't walk
Or talk
Or eat
Or sleep
What else is there to know?
They just mumble
And grumble
And stand all day long
Mummies, mummies, mummies.

# Pie

*by Monica Rasch*

Pie is good to eat
It comes in many different flavors
Pumpkin
Cherry
Apple
And more!!!
Pie is better than cake
At least that's what I think
You can even add toppings
Whip cream
Cherries
Strawberries
Nuts
Or whatever you think
If you haven't tried it
You're missing out
It tastes so delicious
I think you should try it
Because
Pie is good to eat.

# Put it Down

*by Miranda Rios*

You don't have to shove it in your pocket
Or send it in a rocket
Just put it down!

You don't have to put it on a train
Or put it down the drain
Just put it down!

You don't have to lock it in a drawer
Or throw it out the door
Just put it down!

You don't have to send it out of town
Friend, just put it down!

# Rome

*by Miranda Rios*

Rome was a large empire,
Filled with your hearts desires,
But now it's smaller than it was.
Is this just because?

A wealthy Roman meal,
Was always a big deal.
A feast every day,
While their troubles go away.

Slaves were crying,
For people that were dying,
Which is very sad,
And also makes some people mad.

Rome was a great place,
Filled with grace,
But now I know,
Why it had to go.

# Friends

*by Catharine Ryan*

Friends are great!

Your friends are great
And so are mine.

We can have a lot of fun
In a lot of time.

Everybody starts
With loving hearts.

One of my friends
Wears a loving lotion.

It smells like flowers
That was made from a love potion

Friends are not mean
They are quite nice.

They aren't even keen
When they get hit twice.

Friends are great!

# The Great Wall of China

*by Catharine Ryan*

Built upon miles and miles of mountains,
Weathering three thousand years of wind and rain,
Formed into a long dancing dragon.
Made of stone, built high into the sky.
One of the greatest wonders of the world,
The Great Wall of China.
A dream to climb for the young,
And hope to see for the old.
Climb to the top,
Although you are out of breath,
You are an achiever.

# The Ruins

*by Andrew Schrandt*

The ruins the ruins
How they look so old
Their story is untold
Made out of stone and so tall
Who could have built it all.
It wasn't easy building them
The Mayans struggled to make it then
The ruins are now such a sight
To stare at with delight.

# My Dog

*by Andrew Schrandt*

My dog gray and white
Sleeps in my bed every night.
We awake to the bright sunlight
Thinking what a sight.

She is such a great dog to take
She makes no mistakes
She barks a lot and keeps me safe
I love my dog

If I ever had to give her up
I think I would be so sad I'd throw up
Nothing would ever break the bond
Between me and my best friend, my dog.

# Our History

*Mady Scopp*

From ancient tombs
In Egypt,
To the coliseum
In Rome.

From the Great Wall
Of China,
To the Baptismal Pisa Dome.

Form 1969,
In space the first
Flag on a pole.

To eleven caves
 In Israel,
The Dead Sea Scrolls.

# Life

*by Mady Scopp*

Life is a roller coaster
Life is a ride.
There are big waves
There are low tides.
You may win
You may lose.
You may pick
You may choose.
People cheer
People cry.
They are born
They die.
Life.

# Rome

*by Lindsey Thomas*

Rome,
So historical and beautiful.
Rome,
Gladiators fought in the Coliseum.
Rome,
Where the Pope preaches in St. Peter's Basilica.
Rome,
Where the Pantheon was dedicated to all Roman Gods.
Rome,
The capital of a vast empire.
Finally,
Rome,
Where I want to go.

# Autumn to Winter

*by Lindsey Thomas*

Toward the end of fall
The leaves change many colors
Once they fall, we have to haul
All the leaves raked by my brothers.

Then the trees are bare
With nothing to wear
But a fresh blanket of snow
And much wind to blow.

As the heavy snow falls
A thick layer of white
The winter wind calls
Mother nature shows her might.

# Mummy

*by Emily Trecroci*

Dead body, soft tissue, preserved bones
Old bones found for burial
A soul waiting to be reunited with a body
A body on the journey to the after life
Freed from age, poverty and illness
Washed, purified, embalmed and anointed with oil
Ready to meet their Creator.

# If I Were a Flower

*by Emily Trecroci*

If I were a flower, I would
Look up to the sky with my
Blue blowing petals
My strong roots would grab
The soil deep underground
If I were a flower I'd smell
Like a pink, purpleish plant
If I were a flower I would be the
Center of the universe, none to all.

# Pyramids

*by Jacob Young*

Pyramids you are so tall you touch the sky.
Who knows what mysteries lie inside.
You house the tombs of many Pharaohs.
It took very long to build you.

# Christmas is Near

*by Jacob Young*

It's that time of the year
When the snow falls from the sky.
People caroling right outside.
Christmas is near.

It's that time of the year
When kids play outside in the cold wet snow.
When scent of cinnamon and mints in the air.
Christmas is near.

It's that time of the year
When people put their trees up and ornaments on.
Presents wrapped up and under their trees.
Christmas is near.

It's that time of the year
When snowmen in yards with stone eyes and a carrot nose.
Christmas is near.

# Dead Sea Scrolls

*by Samantha Zitzer*

The Dead Sea Scrolls
The original Bible
Written on papyrus, animal skins and copper
Never again will be seen
Half of them are a mystery
Written in many languages
Wish all was intact
Not all compositions were biblical
But no matter what, they are a sight to see
Now come along with me to see these dead sea mysteries
The Dead Sea Scrolls.

# Book Proceeds Scholarship Fund

The students of St. Joseph Catholic Academy are actively engaged in service to others and ehance their educational experience through community service.

As a result, proceeds from this book are being used to create a new scholarship fund for students who need assistance with funding a private education.

As part of St. Joseph's community service requirement, these poets will participate in the scholarship selection process each school year, offering one or more students funding that will cover partial or full tuition for one year.

# St. Joseph Catholic Academy

St. Joseph Catholic Academy is the premier school for kindergarten through 12th grade students. Students flourish in our faith-based environment that fosters academic excellence, high moral standards, and personal responsibility.

- One-to-One laptop program offers each student his or her own personal computer.
- World Languages teach cultural diversity with Chinese, Spanish, Italian, and French offered at every grade level.
- Catholic values are instilled in all aspects of the student experience.
- Personal attention nurtures the unique gifts of every student.
- Students discover their talents and develop confidence through a wide range of extracurricular activities.

Our ultimate goal is to provide our students with an education that integrates the Catholic faith with a strong academic foundation as they become successful, active members of their communities and churches.

St. Joseph Catholic academy will be open for the 2010-2011 school year. For more information, please visit www.kenoshastjoseph.com or call (262) 654-8651.

*The Best Education. The Best Choice.*

St. Joseph Catholic Academy
Grades K-12

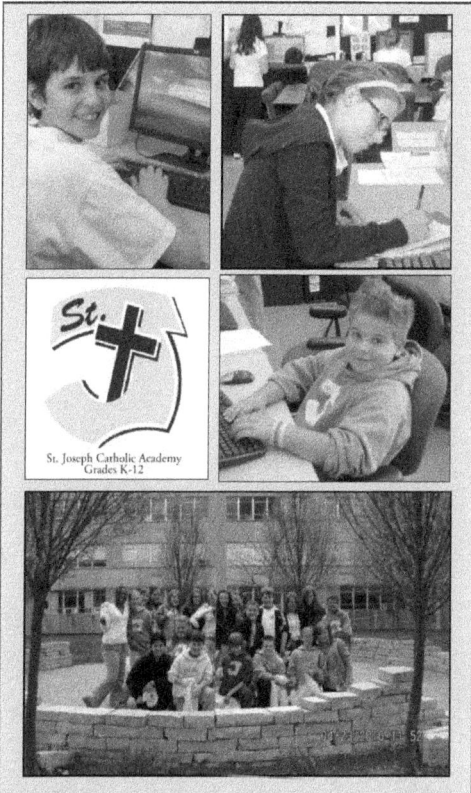

# About Coconut Avenue, Inc.

Coconut Avenue, Inc. is a new publishing company founded in 2008 by Stephen Lesavich, PhD, JD. Coconut Avenue, Inc. is located on LaSalle Street in Chicago, Illinois and publishes creative works that promote soul growth, personal empowerment and self-help, aiming to raise the vibration of our planet.

As part of our ongoing effort to support education and service in our community, Coconut Avenue, Inc. decided to underwrite the costs of publishing this amazing book of poems.

**Stephen Lesavich, PhD, JD**
*Founder, CEO - Coconut Avenue, Inc.*

Chicago, Illinois
June 2010

For more information about Coconut Avenue authors, books, products and events, please contact:

**Coconut Avenue, Inc.**
39 S. LaSalle Street, Suite 325
Chicago, Illinois 60603 USA
312.419.9445 (v)
312.419.9446 (f)
e-mail: info@coconutavenue.com
On-line: coconutavenue.com

**Coconut Avenue®**
The Creative Avenue for Best Selling Authors®
Coconut Avenue,® The Creative Avenue For Best Selling
Authors® and the Coconut Avenue graphic®, are registered
U.S. Trademarks of Coconut Avenue, Inc.